SUCCESS, FAILURE & RECOVERY

75 BUSINESS LESSONS FROM SUCCESSFUL URBAN ENTREPRENEURS

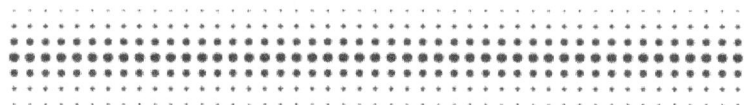

SUCCESS, FAILURE & RECOVERY

75 BUSINESS LESSONS FROM SUCCESSFUL URBAN ENTREPRENEURS

By
Q. Scott Riley

New Guard Multimedia, Inc.
Chicago, Illinois

NEW GUARD
Publishing Division

Success, Failure & Recovery

By: Q. Scott Riley

Copyright © MMVI

New Guard Multimedia, Inc.

Cover Design: Julie M. Holloway
JMH Art & Design Studio
Chicago, IL

JMHCRE8IVE.COM

ISBN Number: 978-0-692-41474-3

Success, Failure & Recovery

Failure is the condiment that gives success its flavor.

~ Truman Capote

Dedication

As a 41-year-old man, there isn't much to ponder as to why I am a teacher, speaker, and writer on the subjects of marketing and entrepreneurship.

If I close my eyes, and imagine myself as a child, standing in front of the house located at 260 E. Sycamore in Kankakee, Illinois.

It's Saturday morning, and just 70 yards east of the front door of my family's house, I can hear the jovial conversation of a group men at Mr. Reed's Car Wash. And, within clear view, I can see a crowd gathering at Marty and Stan's Indiana Ave. Fruit Market at the corner the of block.

As I turn to my left, at the opposite corner, cars are driving in and out of the parking lot of my friend, Jeff Jones' dry cleaners. This is located only half of a block from the funeral home owned by his father, Jefferson Jones, Sr. It is difficult to determine which of those two businesses is the cause for the massive amount of traffic on Schuyler Street.

Or, it is because three of the best barbers in this small town, Robert 'Sonny' Manns, Ira Nelson, and 'Mister' Perry Irving each own and operate barbershops on this same street, within a four block proximity. As I struggle to choose from this array of urban entrepreneurs, to whom I should dedicate this book. I continue to physically turn a full 180 degrees. And now, I face the aforementioned two-story house that is surrounded by this commerce on all sides.

On the inside of the house, is the essence of Urban Entrepreneurship: two Mothers of a local Baptist church are turning their hobbies into a business. Using their God-given talent as an opportunity to enterprise. Mrs. Ruth Riley and her sister Mildred are of cooking fried chicken, collards greens, and potato salad.

In addition to baking Sweet Potato pies, biscuits, and German Chocolate cake, as they await an eager market of 2nd and 3rd shift factory workers, who will soon arrive and purchase the entire inventory.

As I open my eyes to the reality of the present day. I dedicate this book to each of you who were molding and shaping my future unbeknownst to us all, by simply doing what came natural to you. I love you, and I hope that this project will come at least close to being the inspiration to someone, that you are to me.

Ricky White, Owner
Black Eagle Marketing, Inc

Tiffany Jasper, CEO

Carl Ankrum
The Media MD.com

Bryant Thompson, CEO
Red Level Entertainment

Monique Carradine
President, Momentum Media Group

Brian Jenkins
Founder and President
Starting Up Now Business Solutions, Inc.

Atty. Shara Kamal
When Fashion Meets Law PC

Matthew Lee
Homeownership
and Wealth Expert

Shaniqua Jones
Owner, Jements Entertainment

Chef Cordell McGary II
Owner/Executive Chef
Eating Well with Chef Cordell

Julie M. Holloway
Owner, JMH Creative Solutions

Curtis Monday
Agent, State Farm Insurance

Adam Jackson
America's Implementation Expert

Joshua Mercer
Owner, Allstate Insurance Agency

Jason Caston
CEO, Caston Digital LLC

Sherman Wright
Co-Founder/Managing Partner
Commonground

DeAnna McLeary
Founder/Executive Director for
Your Star Foundation

Arika and Monika
Simmons, Double Stitch

Greg Pipkin
Owner, Suburban Tours
and Sports

Ms. Dana
Owner, The Loxticam and Barber Studio

SUCCESS, FAILURE & RECOVERY

75 BUSINESS LESSONS FROM SUCCESSFUL URBAN ENTREPRENEURS

Q. SCOTT RILEY

The Obama Moment

What is the Obama Moment?

"Hello, Chicago...If there is anyone out there who still doubts that America is a place where all things are possible, who still wonders if the dream of our founders is alive in our time, who still questions the power of our democracy, tonight is your answer."

On November 4, 2008, President Barack Obama made that emphatic statement in front of a crowd of thousands in Chicago's Grant Park.

In doing so, he accepted his victory, being elected as President of the United States of America.

In addition, he accomplished what many, for so long, thought was impossible: a black man, elected to be the most powerful person in the free world. That one achievement on the part of a great man, ushered into existence a new reality for a hungry market of urban professionals, which now have proof, they can do anything.

That seminal moment of arrival, was the spark needed for a revolution of urban entrepreneurship. *A moment which*

reached beyond the audacity to hope for new possibilities,
and brought forth the dawn of a new normal.

This was 'The Obama Moment.' And it gave birth to a generation of urban entrepreneurs, comprised of a people who have evolved from boys and girls with ideas, to men and woman with plans.

Contents

Part I. Success

PART I
SUCCESS

Spend as much time as possible learning what you're uniquely talented and gifted at doing.

~ Matthew Lee

SUCCESS

My uncle Joseph once told me, "Quinn, there isn't much difference between courage, and crazy." I often think about that statement whenever I consider the level of courage that is required for one to become an entrepreneur, latter known, a successful one.

Not to mention, anyone would have to be at least a little crazy to attempt to do something that has only a 23% success rate.

And what about those knuckle heads that have an education, as well as, a stable, secure job, and decide to squander it all to pursuit their dream as a business owner.

Imagine the unmitigated nerve of these people who actually believe their plan will work, or that there is a market of consumers out there who will love their idea enough to buy it.

Well my friends that is the essence of entrepreneurship. And I love it! I encourage every living soul to attempt some form of business ownership at least once in their lifetime. There is no greater reward, than to have the creative freedom to earn a living, doing what you love.

Some will argue, "Business ownership isn't for everyone." I say, that is debatable. Have we forgotten, just a few generations ago, this nation's economy and workforce were heavily dependent upon the ingenuity of entrepreneurs who were both crazy and courageous enough to believe in new ideas such as, the Model-T; the disposable razor; the ballpoint pen; a national chain of pizza delivery franchises; and a 24-hour news channel.

And that goes double for an urban market of African Americans who faced historical discrimination and disenfranchisement. As a result, in an effort to create economic viability in their community, were forced to birth ventures such as a cement company, when there was no government aid to buy bricks to build a much needed college for black students. And it even inspired a Detroit-factory worker to turn an abandoned photography studio, into a music recording studio, and created a sound that brought an entire industry to its knees.

So, what happened...where has this Diaspora of crazy ingenuity, and cultural courage gone?

Beginning in the early 1970's, the spoils of victory accomplished by the Civil Rights Movement a decade prior, included a boom of corporate, middle-class career opportunities for a generation of qualified black professionals. Who were ready to join the ranks of the corporate world.

Thus, creating a cultural shift, and the roots of equity and ownership, were traded in exchange for the fruit of commercial acceptance. Legendary, Atlanta-based businessman, Herman J. Russell, said,"...there's a generation in which entrepreneurship was not emphasized-- just white collar jobs. We have to realize entrepreneurship made black white-collar workers possible."

Now, allow me to be unmistakably clear. There is absolutely nothing wrong with a good job. Nothing! But what happens when middle class America is continuously being "automated, downsized, and outsourced," as Thomas Friedman points out in his bestseller, *The World is Flat*.

To that end, I believe Whitney Young said it best, "We may have come over on different ships, but we are now all in the same boat."

In large part, Part I of this book, *Success*, is intended to dispel the myth about entrepreneurship that causes many to avoid it. That myth says, business ownership is a monolith. It is not.

As this book will illustrate, entrepreneurship has various levels of experiences, ranging from being a hobbyist, to being Self Employed, to becoming a business owner. The reasons for starting a business venture vary as well.

A good example of that point is my mentor, Cuttie Bacon, III, PhD. Early in his career, Dr. Bacon was looking for a way to supplement his salary as a high school teacher.

So he decided to drive a city bus at night. He then invested all of his bus driver earnings into income properties, and eventually became a very successful real estate mogul.

On the other hand, there are experiences such as that of Arika and Monika Simmons.

Twin sisters who one year, chose to make crochet clothing designs for their family and friends as Christmas gifts. Upon giving the gifts away, they learned there was a demand from people who were willing to purchase their products.

They were inspired to start their own clothing line, and the rest is history...

Thus, entrepreneurship should not be looked upon simply as a risky endeavor, or something set aside for the wealthy and privileged. Instead it should be embraced as a culture, a mentality, and a viable career alternative.

My friend, business owner, Ken Castleberry surmised it well, when he advised, "Entrepreneurship is one of the surest ways you can depend on money to pay your mortgage, buy groceries, and send your kids to school. Without worrying about another person's decision, making or breaking your ability to do any of those things."

So, how does a predominately African American, urban consumer market, that is worth $1 trillion turn itself inside out, and benefit from the trends and industries that this same market can be credited with creating?
The answer is entrepreneurship.

At this point, undoubtedly the concerns of risk and success rates become the primary question.

Look at this way, in this life there are risk factors related to everything: 46% of first-time college students will drop out. 50% of first-time marriages in America will end in divorce. And in 2012, the U.S. economy experienced an unemployment rate of 10%...

But there must be a formula that breeds success for some, where others fail. Because 54% of college students complete their studies. And what about the 50% of married couples who stay together. What do they know that others do not? In the words of filmmaker, Woody Allen, 'It's like anything else.'

And I submit that attaining success as an entrepreneur is like anything else.

If there are individuals, who are alive and well, and have reached success as business owners, why not simply ask them for their formula? And that is exactly what I did.

Twenty-four successful urban entrepreneurs, were interviewed and asked, "Which business strategies have you used to achieve success, and would encourage others to repeat?"

Which business strategies have you used to achieve success, and would encourage others to repeat?

LESSON #1

Study the Habits of Successful People

Monique Caradine, President, Momentum Media Group

"The most important thing you can do as an entrepreneur is to create a daily routine that breeds success." That's what I teach my clients. I have personally become a student of success over the past five years. And I've learned it is critical to study the mindsets of the most successful people in the world. The stories are out there, and easy to get.

There is no need to reinvent the wheel, the formula already exist. Anything you're interested in knowing: how they think, how they behave, what their habits are, what they do on a daily basis, how they start their day, how they end their day, etc. Simply identify the people you admire the most, who have experience success at the greatest levels.

After you create your list, study them. Learn and emulate their habits. These are things you need to learn before you start your business. However, you should also include the entrepreneurs who have failed at the greatest levels as well. You can't have great success without failure.

The things you do everyday speak to the level of success that you create for your future. If you're not where you want to be, or you don't have what you want in business and in life. All you have to do, to figure out why you're not there, is look at what you do only on a daily basis.

Purchase a copy of
Harvey Mackay's book, Fired Up!

LESSON #2

Create Plans that Complement Your Goals

Tiffany Jasper, CEO, Tiff's Editing Cafe

The success strategy I would suggest for entrepreneurs is to adopt a long-term mentor or business coach. And surround yourself with innovative thinkers, who are successful business men and women. However, although positive business relationships are good to have. Be sure to create tangible, daily to-do lists that are relevant to your individual business goals.

It is every business owner's dream, to achieve success in the industry they have chosen. But, it is critical to understand that each path to success may differ. This often calls for unique, specific tactics and ways of reaching our goals.

No one has the perfect route to success, for everyone. Therefore, you must choose the best practices that fit the business and the lifestyle you want.

Purchase a copy of
Brian Tracy's book, Success Guide

LESSON #3

Don't Give Up!

Carl Ankrum, The Media MD.com

I would encourage all entrepreneurs to never give up. Personal experience has taught me, there will always be things present to discourage you. For example, as entrepreneurs, we will all face rejection. And when that happens, learn to be at peace with it. You are not going to be the right vendor for every market, or for that matter, for every individual. You won't be the right photographer, cook, barber, or designer to meet the needs of every potential customer.

Remember, promote your business to the general market, and receive the customers that appreciate you and what you have to offer. And if it takes longer than you anticipated to find your customer base, do everything within your power to not get discouraged. Even when business slows down, don't give up, don't give up, and don't give up!

You face your greatest opposition, when you're closest to your biggest miracle.

~ T. D. Jakes

LESSON #4

Maintain Close Relationships with Industry People

Shara Kamal, Founder/Managing Attorney,
When Fashion Meets Law, PC

It is important to maintain close relationships with the right people in your industry. This will enable you to educate yourself on the needs of your clients. Continuously staying abreast on what's happening in the world, and how any changes might affect your customers, will allow you to modify your services and products in an effort serve your market, as an ongoing resource.

Also, study other industries that may affect your industry. That will enable you to make adjustments in the proper timeframe, so that your business is not harmed as a result of indirect changes. In addition, develop solid relationships with your clients. It's not always about the deal, or one transaction, but really more about valuing the importance of the business-to-client relationship.

Therefore, surround yourself with like minded individuals. People who have 'been there and done that.' It is invaluable to have an extra set of experienced eyes to review your plan. I grew up within a family of entrepreneurs, and I've learned to appreciate how vital it is, to find a group of people you can trust, who will be honest with you, while at the same time encourage you.

If you don't love the business, you won't succeed as an entrepreneur...

~ Sean Hicks

LESSON #5

Do What You Love!

Sean Hicks, Principal/Chief Creative Officer, Gargoyle Creative Designs

As an entrepreneur, what ever you choose, its got to be something you love. The business can not be something out of your box, or out of your wheelhouse. Any venture that you choose, and expect to achieve any degree of success, will be formed within the realm of your own creative nature.

For example, my son, as a kindergartener, decided to start a business. Quite naturally, he was drawn to something that he saw everyone else doing on TV...selling lemonade.

So I challenged him, and asked, "Do you like making lemonade?" To which he replied, "No." I then asked him, "Well what do you really like to do?" He said, "I really like playing with my dog." I said, "Well then, take some time and think about how you can create a business, working with dogs." He said, "what about dog treats?" So, he placed three Alpo dog treats in a plastic bag, (in a neighborhood where people often walk their dogs) and sold them for .50 cents per bag.

On his first day, he sold 25 bags, and got tips. His first day of business, as a 5-year-old, he walked away with over $30 in profits. The following week, he expanded the business, and recruited a couple of his friends, and they went door-to-door, and sold an additional 50 bags.

The moral is, what ever you do, if you want to succeed, make sure you enjoy doing it. Lets say you choose to be an author, and start a business, self-publishing books.

But suddenly, you decide to bake and sell cakes on the side. If writing is your passion, that cake business will only last until you get tired. Because one day, you're not going to feel like baking, and you're going to quit. For that reason, you need to choose an entrepreneurial venture that drives and motivates you.

What ever you put your name on as a business owner, make sure you enjoy it. Do not do it, for the sake of doing it.

Believe it or not, it doesn't make a difference how much potential money can be made. If you don't love the business, you won't succeed as an entrepreneur.

LESSON #6

Find Your Unique Gift

Matthew Lee, 'America's Homeownership and Wealth Expert'

In life, we are naturally drawn to what we are uniquely gifted at doing. Thus, I would suggest entrepreneurs to repeat, what I call, my magic formula for success: 'spend as much time as possible learning what you're uniquely talented and gifted at doing.'

However, that process can be one that includes the undoing of lifelong lessons that are counterproductive to an entrepreneurial spirit. For example, consider artists, such as Kevin Hart. Who is arguably the hottest comedian in the market right now. He has been a naturally funny person his entire life. Although as a child and student, he was regularly chided as a result of his unique gift. But eventually he decided to use that gift to his advantage. Therefore, he had to undo the effect of the messages that he had been told throughout his life.

The number one thing entrepreneurs should do is discover their unique talents and capabilities, and then begin to build their business on that discovery, as a foundation. The best way to discover your unique gift is to ask 10-15 people who you've worked with, 'what are the skills or talents that you would come to me for?'

Often times we don't recognize our own gifts, in the same way a fish would take water for granted. He's always around it. Therefore, it may take an outside person, who is not gifted as we are in a particular area, to help us identify, and appreciate the skills and gifts we possess.

The next step is to develop a team of other people who have skills in the areas where you are weak.

Avoid trying to be Mr. or Mrs. do-it-all in the market. Highlight the things you do very well, and do them. That is what separates the Steve Jobs, the Mark Zuckerbergs, and the Bill Gates from the crowd.

More than being just very smart in their area of specialty, they build a team around them, consisting of people who have gifts and talents in areas, where they do not.

Successful entrepreneurship goes beyond strengthening your weaknesses. If you focus on just strengthening your weaknesses, you'll just have a bunch of strong weaknesses. Successful entrepreneurship requires un-doing the effect our weaknesses have on us.

LESSON #7

KISS: Keep it Simple Stupid

Brian Jenkins, L. Brian Jenkins, President/Founder, Starting Up Now Business Solutions, Inc.

As a business owner, you must stay focused on your company's mission and vision. Beware, there will always be people who will come along with new ideas and changes, and have no operation model to accomplish their suggestions.

Do not be distracted by sideways energy, whether it is in the form of people, systems, or opportunities.

Even if it is something as simple as upgrading the latest version of your operation system. Take the time to ask yourself these questions, 'Is this really necessary?' 'Does this fit within my original mission statement?'
I think it is important to have a copy of your mission statement written on paper, on your desk, in front of you at all times. This is particularly important, as your company

and team grow. Again, you will encounter people who have lots of ideas, and no execution models.

In those moments, you have to remain focused on what you're trying to accomplish. And, as the owner of the company, you must set the tone of focus.

LESSON #8

Establish Your Legal Structure, ASAP

Julie Holloway, President, JMH Art + Design Studio

The strategy I would suggest entrepreneurs to repeat is to establish your legal structure, brand, and operation process, prior to launching your business. I say that because these are the three most critical areas that can make or break, your ability to earn a profit as an entrepreneur.

These are the things you need to have in place before you start piling on the customers. And they need to be in place for many reasons, including protecting your company, yourself, and your brand.

I say that in hindsight, because I took my hobby and turned it into a business. But when I think about it now, I know that I did that much, too fast. I didn't stop and take the time to consider things, such as those three components, as much as I would have liked.

So now, I'm a couple of years into business ownership, and when I look at some of those areas of the company, I say to myself, "I wish I would have done this first!"

LESSON #9

Prepare a Peak Performance Manual

Adam Jackson, 'America's Implementation Expert'

I encourage all entrepreneurs to remember, 'proper preparation prevents poor performance.' So often, I find that many people, business owners included, fail to prepare for greatness in the areas where they want to achieve mastery.

Let's say for instance, you buy a car. Within that car there is supposed to be an operation manual. If in any case the car malfunctions in one way or another, i.e., a light comes on the dashboard, a sensor goes bad, or an unusual noise repeats.

The owner can refer to the manual and figure out the problem. Likewise, a business should have an operation manual, as well. It's called an executive summary or business plan. A business plan is set up for success, not failure. If you ever experience failure in your business, you should be able to refer to the business plan or executive summary, and figure where you went wrong.

It is catastrophic in entrepreneurship when business owners launch a business without having any form of preparation in writing.

LESSON #10

Take Risk

Chef Cordell McGary, II Owner/Executive Chef, Eating Well with Chef Cordell

Don't be afraid to take a risk. So often, entrepreneurs take the time to prepare a formula to do business, but fail to listen that message from their inner-self, that says, 'actually start the business.'

Although research and being informed are paramount, you must follow your heart. Some times you may have viable business idea, and things aren't going as well as you planned or hoped, and it may start to feel risky...but keep going.

If your vision is clear and your goals are attainable, don't quit. It is critical to stay in the game, avoid quitting at all costs. As soon as you stop, it's over!

LESSON #11

Study to Show Thyself Approved

Curtis Monday, Agent, State Farm Insurance

I think that all business owners, prior to taking the plunge into whatever endeavor they choose, should do as much homework as possible. All entrepreneurs should study, to show thyself approved. Before you launch a venture, ask yourself these important questions, "What are the risks?" "What are the possibilities?" "Are there any companies that are doing well in that industry?" "How did they do it?"

When you start your business, have good people around you. As an entrepreneur, you can't go far without the right people in your presence. Therefore, it is a good idea to develop your people skills, and learn how to motivate, lead, and manage people.

As a business owner, you have to learn how to work through people. How to translate your energy, communicate your message, and share your passion. It is important to be able to get others to appreciate the process that comes with every promise.

Not every person thinks that way. But as the leader, you have to emphasize to others, the importance of a business going from promise to process.

LESSON #12

Fortify Your Business

Q. Scott Riley, CEO, New Guard Multimedia

Fortify your business against known fears, and concerns. In other words, think about things that you feel could go wrong. Then create a list of those potential problems, and do your best to solve them before they occur.

There are two efficient ways to do the aforementioned. 1) Form a group comprised of 10 trustworthy business associates, and ask each person, based on their experience, to analyze your plan, and give you two things that they feel could be problematic within your business.

2) Do a SWOT analysis for your business of choice. A SWOT analysis will enable you to identify strengths, weaknesses, opportunities, and threats related to your business within your market and industry.

LESSON #13

Create a Personal Internship

Arika and Monika Simmons, Double Stitch

(Monika Simmons) I've learned that the three most important things in entrepreneurship are, research, research, and research! So often, people will come up a business idea, without doing any research. I find it to be hilarious, that any person would think in this day and age, that they are so smart, that no one else has come close to thinking about a similar idea. Really! No one is that smart. The key is to throw yourself into a world of what you're interested in doing.

Find groups of people who gather and discuss the type of business you're interested in. They will have access to resources related to your idea. Furthermore, engulf yourself into your industry by doing your own personal internship. As an entrepreneur, my best experiences came from going to industry events, and dabbling into every opportunity I could find, that was related to my business.

When I was trying to get my products sold at major stores such as Macy's, and other places, I was going from fashion show to fashion show, and from event to event. And it didn't seem like work, because it was the nature of the business we chose. I had to learn how people who were already established in my industry operated their business.

But, honestly, if someone had given me a syllabus, and told me that these are the things you should research for the next 12-20 months, before you open your business. I would have said, 'you're crazy, and there's no way I'm doing that.'

But, that is exactly what I did, and I had fun doing it. Entrepreneurs should make a commitment to create a fun, personal internship for themselves, during their research phase.

If I could go back in time, and start all over again. I think I would fine tune my business, once a month.

~ Ms. Dana

LESSON #14

Be Flexible

Ms Dana, Owner, The Loctician and Barber Studio

In light of everything that others may say about the business plan, the importance of mentorship, surrounding yourself with like-minded people, and don't give up... For entrepreneurs, having flexibility to change is often overlooked, and underrated. Therefore, a key strategy for all entrepreneurs, that is worthy of repeating. Be flexible!

If I could go back and start all over again, I think I would fine tune my business once a month. I often share with my mentors, or even think to myself, "If I took and changed this, that can work better. Or, if I by doing that, I could work more efficiently."

I've learned that business is not all about one continuous flow of productivity. Things can and will change. And when they do, you will want to throw everything in the air and walk away. Don't!

That's when you need to call someone on the phone and just get that B-12 shot of encouragement that your heart and soul so desperately need. This is especially true when you fail. And we all will at some point. But, it is in those moments, you need to have focus, tenacity, and be flexible to change.

You don't have to have a million dollars to look like a million dollar company.

~ Jason Caston

LESSON #15

Perception is Everything

Jason Caston, CEO, Caston Digital LLC

The main success strategy that I would encourage entrepreneurs to remember is that perception is everything. Even if you don't have a million dollars in revenues...you don't have to have a million dollars, to look like a million dollar company.

But you have to be mindful of the perception of your business. So, the question becomes, where can you improve, with the money you have? The strategy is to make your business look like it's much more professional than it actually is.

Consider this, when you go into a restaurant –and the food is great and so is the service, after the meal is over, you leave the restaurant and think, everything is fine with that business. But you have no idea what is going on in the kitchen!

It is critical for the perception of any business to look like a professional, well run company. A good example of that would be your company's website.

If your website looks like a Fortune 500 company, then no matter what else is going on—the perception of your business is that it is a Fortune 500 company. That's the perception.

LESSON #16

Maintain Integrity within Your Market

Joshua Mercer, Owner, Allstate Insurance Agency

Always have integrity, because your reputation will mean almost everything. Maintain integrity, not only with business associates, but with your community, and with your customers. As an entrepreneur, you work for your customers—you have to remember they are number one.

Also, I would definitely say always continue to expand your network of people. You want to identify people who are successful, and are in those circles so that some of that success can rub off on you.

But before entering those circles, people will require you to have a certain level of character and integrity.

LESSON #17

Ignore the Peanut Gallery

Richard White II, CEO, Black Eagle Marketing, Inc.

Don't be afraid change industries if think you see an opportunity to make money doing something else. As entrepreneurs, we get comfortable far too soon, and aren't always in the best position to do so. And don't worry about what others may say if you switch industries. Know your own worth, and continue to learn from making mistakes, and by trying different things.

LESSON #18

Remove the Box

Shaniqua Jones, Owner, Senorita Entertainment

Fight the temptation to limit yourself. Don't just think outside of the box, remove the box. As an entrepreneur, you should completely move away from that concept. Just the idea alone, suggest that there is a box. So throw the box away.

If you have passion and determination, your passion will make room for you. Therefore, think of how you can develop a sustainable business that can stand the test of time; one that will withstand hardships, and obstacles.

But, don't throw caution completely to the wind, and underestimate the importance of research. Sometimes when we have passion or great ideas, we don't ask the key question, 'What does the outcome look like?' The discoveries of your research will answer that question, and remove the limits.

LESSON #19

The 5 P's of Entrepreneurship

Sherman Wright, Co-Founder/Managing Partner, Common Ground

The strategy for success I find that works me, and would tell entrepreneurs to assure themselves with, is what I call the 5 P's of the entrepreneurial journey. And they are: 1) passion 2) preparation 3) persistence 4) patience and 5) prayer. I feel, that no matter what entrepreneurial venture you decide to pursue, all those things will come into play.

That passion, that preparation, that persistence, that patience, and that sense of faith, prayer. I think those things will allow you to know who you are as an entrepreneur.

It's not about your past accomplishments, or what you want to do in the future, it's about who you are as a person in regards to meeting the challenges and adversity that you are going to face as an entrepreneur. As well as, how you are going to interact and treat those you work with, not only in the good times, but even in the bad times.

It's important to know how to properly respond when things don't go as planned. That is the test. How do you respond when you're faced with adversity? How do you respond to the challenges that entrepreneurship brings, when things are not going well? That is the key to understanding who you are as an entrepreneur.

LESSON #20

The 3 T's of Entrepreneurship: test, test, test!

Warren Dobson, Dobson Products

In entrepreneurship, everything is a test. Until its not! In other words, each and everything a business owner plans to do, whether it is marketing, partnerships, new products, suppliers, etc. It is all a test, until the method proves to be successful.

LESSON #21

Discover Ways to Work Smarter, Not Harder

Bryant Thompson, CEO, Red Level Entertainment

I have repeatedly employed two strategies within my business and found consistent success. The first is simple: Be sure at all times you are working towards increasing your assets, and minimizing your liabilities. Assets generate profits, while liabilities do the opposite.

The second strategy is creating systems that will allow you to work smarter, and not harder.

Discover as many ways as possible to outsource, batch, and automate your business operations.

Purchase a copy of
Tim Ferriss' book,
The Four Hour Work Week

LESSON #22

Distinguish Your Brand to the Market

Greg Pipkin, Owner, Suburban Tees and Sports

The strategy I would encourage small business owners to repeat, in an effort to increase their potential for success, is to recognize who you are in the market. The first lesson to remember is that you are your business. The relationships you develop with your clients early on are critical to your brand.

Therefore, recognize and realize that you're not going to sell your products to everyone. Understanding this principle early on will help you to avoid becoming a fad or trend.

For example, when I was in high school, there were certain clothing brands that were hottest trends on the market. But in just a matter of a few years, they each fazed out. What happened? What was the difference between those brands, and others such as Ralph Lauren that has stood the test of time?

67

The difference is the rapport an entrepreneur has with the market. That is going to be the driving force behind your brand. Fact is, very few strong brands just pop up over night.

I know I'm a small business in a big field, and there are bigger companies that may be able to offer lower prices. So I don't try to compete in that area of the market. Instead, I know who I am in my market. And as a small business owner, I compete in areas such as personal touch. My customers can actually meet and shake the hand of the person who is doing the work.

So, as your business grows, it is important to maintain the qualities that allowed you gain the initial attention of your market.

Lesson #23

Become an Employee of Your Business

DeAnna McLeary, Founder/Executive Director, True Star Foundation

Pay yourself, professionally! I learned personally, from a financial expert, how wrong it is to just simply pull cash from a business account, and pay for personal items, such as rent, groceries, etc. Unless you are self employed, that is a bad practice.

But if you own a business that requires overhead, which includes employees, office space, materials, and utilities...don't make a habit of pulling money out of the cash register. As a business owner, setup a professional system.

When I decided to do that, it changed my ideology regarding business ownership. When you put yourself on salary, it changes your professional perspective, and it becomes a natural feeling as an owner.

Initially, because it's your business, you may feel that if you made the sacrifices, and the investment of sweat equity, then you're not doing anything wrong, to simply take the company's credit or debit card, and spend it on something you need. After all, it's your money, right? Wrong!

Put yourself on a salary that the business can afford. At that point you will have a regular pay roll to manage. This practice will also force a business owner to pay more attention to cash flow, which is something you should do anyway.

LESSON #24

Give Back Before You Gain

Ms Dana, Owner, The Loctician and Barber Studio

We may think since we're still building that we don't have anything to give. Or, we may believe that, since we are not where we want to be, how can we help others? As entrepreneurs, we always have something to give, and once we make that a habit, then reaching our successes will become more than we ever dreamed.

My mother once said of Oprah Winfrey, Bill Gates, and Warren Buffet, "They wouldn't have anything close to what they have, if it weren't for their giving." When you think about it, they are all in different industries. But as three of the wealthiest people in this country, the one common denominator is that they give.

Look at Oprah--she talks other people into giving. A lot of people don't realize that fact, and they actually think she bought all that stuff on her "favorite things show."

No, her staff calls and talks companies into giving the stuff away. We may think we don't have anything to give, but we always have something to give that will contribute to someone else. This subject means so much to me, because when I began as an entrepreneur, I failed so much in my attempts to find people who were willing to help me. I'm definitely not going to give names because that is the sad part about my story, but it worked out for my good.

In the personal grooming industry, it was hard for me to find mentors. People didn't want to give me information, and I don't know if it was the fear of competition, or if it's just the stinginess of information.

I vowed that I would break that industry trend of hoarding information, if I ever got the chance. My first opportunity came when I finally reached a point in my industry, Natural Hair Care, that people would consider me as a reference source. And as they began coming to me for advice, I gave it freely. Once, I mentored a young lady who had experienced the same thing I had--no one would give her advice. She and I spoke over the phone, and one point, I thought the phone went dead, but it didn't.

She was still on the call, but she was so stunned by the amount of information I willingly offered her, she did not know how to respond. I knew then, I was nowhere near where I wanted to be. I'm still not, but I had something to give. I'm not doing it to be Oprah, Bill, or Warren. I just want to make sure that when someone comes along behind me, they won't hit the brick wall that I did. Not if I'm the one they reach out to.

What I've learned firsthand is that mentorship is not a time vacuum. You can be strategic and pour into someone incredibly, in a 30-60 minute time slot.

Give, and it shall be given unto you; good measure, pressed down, and shaken together, and running over, shall men give into your bosom.
Luke 6:38

Part II
Failure

"Your actuality does not have to become your reality."

~ Adam Jackson

FAILURE

As an entrepreneur, business can be a win-win experience. In other words, even when all circumstances indicate that you're failing, you can still find a formula for success in the midst.

Most often, when we are successful as business owners, we measure in terms of growth, gain, and profiting. However, many entrepreneurs are unaware of a little known, yet important fact. The same growth, gain, and profits we experience during seasons of success, can be accomplished through our failures as well. The only difference is that the outcomes may appear in forms that are not typically included in a business plan, or on a vision board.

Nevertheless, the gains from failure can be equally valuable as those garnered by success to an entrepreneur in the long run. Some would argue the former carries an even greater importance than the latter. Though during what may be perceived as a period of failure, the manifestation of our return on investment may surprisingly show up as character, wisdom, or connections. Instead of dividends, publicity, or sales.

Still, anyone planning to be a successful entrepreneur must embrace the fact, that failure is an intractable part of success.

Bill Gates said, "Success is a lousy teacher. It makes smart people believe they can't fail." On the contrary, I have learned that failure can be your best friend, or your worst enemy. The choice is yours. Too often, after failing, many entrepreneurs quit. Big mistake!

A small town newspaper printer quit his job one day, after deciding that printing was not the right profession for him.

He later got a job at a candy factory in Lancaster, Pennsylvania. After working a few years at the candy factory, he decided to open his own little candy business near Philadelphia.

Alas, his first business had to close down because it was not making any money. After closing down his first business, he traveled to Denver, Colorado, to learn how to make caramels.

He eventually took his new skills to New York and worked selling candies on the street. But that second business also failed.

Finally, this frustrated entrepreneur moved back to the farm hills of Pennsylvania where he grew up. He then experimented with all sorts of different candies and chocolates. The area where he lived had lots and lots of dairy farms, so he had a large and easy supply of fresh milk.

And when he couldn't afford many supplies, such as sugar, Milton Hershey discovered how to make delicious chocolate by using fresh, sweet condensed milk...

After tasting the bitter, bile-like flavor of failure as an entrepreneur for the first time, the next question you will hear from the depths of your conscience is, "How much do you really want this?"

Here is the good news. Past failure is the blueprint of future success. It is your medal of honor for experience.

But please make sure, when you fail, to swallow your pride, and do not equate failure to finality. Failure does not mean the end.

Let's consider an interesting contrast: success rates. The success rate of first time entrepreneur is only 23%.

However, the success rate of entrepreneurs who failed, and decided to try again, is 78%. In other words, roughly 8-out-of-10 entrepreneurs will fail their first try.

But the success rate more than triples, on the second try, for those who fail, learn, and re-launch.

The saddest part of this data is, of the eight entrepreneurs who fail the first time; only two will attempt a new venture.

That means six business owners walked away, and allowed their pride to overshadow the knowledge and experience that failure offers us! Are you one failure away from your dreams?

Part II of this book, *Failure*, will teach the reader three key principles of entrepreneurship: 1) How to embrace failure. 2) How not to misunderstand failure as a problem, but to receive it as a part of the process. 3) How to gain knowledge from the mistakes made by others.

Twenty-four successful urban entrepreneurs, were interviewed and asked, "As a business owner, which critical mistakes have you experienced, that you would advise all entrepreneurs to avoid?"

As a business owner, which critical mistakes have you experienced, that you would advise all entrepreneurs to avoid?

LESSON #25

Don't Under Estimate Start Up Costs

Greg Pipkin, Owner, Suburban Tees and Sports

Don't under estimate start up expenses. This is a mistake that I made personally. Within your initial plan, you may think of things like computers, and software, etc. But did you think of data storage?

For example, I use Google Docs, and that's only $3 per month. However, if you multiply $3 times 12 months, that's $36 per year. That may not seem like much, but if it was not in your initial budget, that can be a problem later.

And there can be a hundred little expenses like that which add up, fast! Such as business cards. You may purchase the first box of cards, but you have to keep in mind, that for every card you give out, that brings you closer to buying a new box, and incurring a new expense. So be sure you know the operating costs, and how much it really cost to run your business on a monthly basis. Always overestimate your projected cost to operate a business.

LESSON #26

Don't Over Promise and Under Perform

L. Brian Jenkins, President/Founder, Starting Up Now Business Solutions, Inc.

The best way to avoid the mistake of over promising, is continuously asking yourself the question, "How can I create the 'wow' factor?" For example, if you were selling writing pens and a customer ordered 100 units. You should add five additional pens.

If it doesn't seriously crush your profit margin, where is the harm? Particularly, if the customer will remember that you exceeded the minimal of their expectations.

Don't promise the world, and fall short on the deliverables of your core components. Always do the exact opposite of that--under promise and over perform.

LESSON #27

Don't Believe Your Own Hype

Matthew Lee, 'America's Homeownership and Wealth Expert'

Get rid of your ego! Although, it does take a large amount of courage to become an entrepreneur, and you don't often find shy people among the crowd, it is still important to keep your ego in check.

Most business owners are very proactive, go-getters, who are constantly receiving praise, awards, pats on the back, accolades, etc.

Therefore, we tend to build a sense of extreme self worth and confidence, often times to our own demise. People will look at you as if you're bigger than life, which can cause us to sometimes not assess problems that are on the horizon.

Although the indicators are there, we're so high and mighty, we couldn't see them, or ignored them. Entrepreneurs by nature have thick skin. They do their own thing, and care very little about the opinions of others, and feel as though they can conquer anything in their way. This can be a good thing for a business owner...almost necessary.

However, when the entrepreneur's ego completely takes over, and starts to tell the business owner their stuff don't stink, that person can drown in their own hype. So, again, keep your ego in check.

LESSON #28

Avoid Becoming a Jack-of-All Trade

Carl Ankrum, The Media MD.com

Quite often, I have considered, whether I should have stayed in one specific area of the media industry. There is an old familiar quote, 'A Jack-of-all-trades. Master of none.' I would encourage small business owners to avoid doing that.

In fact, I would encourage all entrepreneurs to avoid getting into too many different professional fronts, even if they are in the same industry. When I started my business, I focused on sound engineering. But media is a broad profession with many different areas, offering many different opportunities.

And at one time, I was trying to do them all (graphics, websites, etc.). But, I learned you have to let some things go. And stay more focused on what you're good at.

Do not get lost trying to get into things that you clearly should not pursue. I learned that lesson through personal experience. I would be a lot further in the sound engineering sector, if I had focused, and taken advantage of educational and training opportunities in that particular area of my field. This would have led to bigger opportunities, sooner.

In addition, don't jump on opportunities that you know you should not do, just because cash flow is slow. So often, entrepreneurs will try to do jobs that are close to their trade, in an effort to make up for periods of slow sales. Even though they know that is not their expertise.

Thus, they will lower the price for the services that they are less familiar with, almost as a bonus. But by doing this, you take yourself out of your wheel house, and as a result, offer subpar results to the client. I have made the aforementioned mistake in the past, and I felt bad because I knew I did not deliver my best work. So, I discounted the price significantly, which caused the business to lose money, and was an unnecessary waste of time.

Never be afraid of the
size of your gift.

~ Monique Caradine

LESSON #29

Don't Play Small

Monique Caradine, President, Momentum Media Group

When I started my business, I could have leveraged the name recognition I already had, as a radio personality, in major market. But I think I down played the size of the gift I had. And because I was afraid of the size of my gift, I was afraid of the size of the success it could offer.

Unfortunately, I didn't own my gift. I learned, it is a dangerous thing to play it small. As an entrepreneur, never be afraid of the size of your gift. If you have a big presence, and can offer a big solution to a problem, you have to own that.

Profit always follows value. Clearly articulate the value of your gift, and be crystal clear about what your have to offer to people. If I would have been able to articulate my value, I would have been far more successful, and profitable.

Furthermore, avoid not understanding the value of marketing. You have to find ways to let the market know your value. That's your brand. You are the embodiment of your brand, so you can't afford to play small. Show up and show up big! Remember, your market value is the ability to articulate your value proposition.

The moment you stop looking for new clients, is the moment your business stops being your top priority...

~ Sean Hicks

LESSON #30

Never Lose Your Hustle

Sean Hicks, Principal/Chief Creative Officer, Gargoyle Creative Designs

In my opinion, the biggest mistake an entrepreneur can make, is having a good year, and then, stop hustling. Even worse, to stop looking for the next client. What happens when your current best client changes their mind, and decides to go elsewhere? Or, what happens when there is a change within your client's operation, and they can't continue to purchase your services? Or, if you have a major conflict with a customer, and the best thing for all parties is to dissolve the business relationship. What happens then?

If this happens, it possible for your clientele to decline from six core, repeat customers, to just two. And the first place you feel that is on your books. You can find yourself going from grossing over $100,000/year, to just above $15,000/year.

After you realize that, you begin to make the effort to find new clients right away, to replace the revenue you've lost. And that is dangerous. Therefore, do not stop the hustle. Always continue to promote and market, and don't ever get comfortable.

Avoid the temptation to relax and host a bar-b-que every time it looks as if your business is doing well. If you have to, turn business away, but never quit looking for it.

It is always a good problem to have more business than you can handle, than not enough. The moment you stop looking for new clients, is the moment your business stops being your top priority.

Action has no season.

~ Shara Kamal

LESSON #31

Fight Against the Fear of Making Your Move

Shara Kamal, Founder/Managing Attorney, When Fashion Meets Law, PC

Some mistakes we are supposed to make, they are necessary. Because all the advice in the world will not replace the experience a business owner can gain from making his/her own personal mistakes. Some of my clients come to me after doing all sorts research; going to free workshop after workshop, and doing so much investigating on the subject of a new technology, or how to take advantage of a fresh idea.

But their mistake is that they fail to take action. And by the time make their move, someone else has taken advantage of that market opportunity. Action has no season. There is only so much research and investigating you can afford to do. It is fine to invest in good counsel, do the focus groups, etc. But you have to take action at some point, timing is key.

Real estate investing is a prime example, I have clients who come to me, and want to do a lot of unnecessary due diligence, and I tell them, '"This is a buyers market; you don't want to miss the boat." Even if you make mistakes, that's why you have counsel. The bigger mistake is not being in action, not making the deal.

LESSON #32

Remove Arrogance from Your Business

Adam Jackson, 'America's Implementation Expert'

In the year 2000, I went from traveling in private jets, and owning time-shares, to filing for a $1.5 million bankruptcy. Why did that happen? Because I purchased a retail clothing store and decided to sell the products that I thought were hot. The things that I felt were trendy. These decisions were based solely on my own assumptions and arrogance. I did not do market and demographic research to determine what the market's real demands were.

However, last year, I was part of a self reflection/ empowerment speaking tour. And the topic I spoke on was this: 'The key to success is to set self aside within all that you do.'

For example, in a personal relationship or marriage, if you make the relationship about the mate, and remove arrogance, and selfishness, eventually, your efforts will reciprocate back to you. The same is true in business.

LESSON #33

Don't Go Against Your Gut, for a Quick Buck

Chef Cordell McGary, II Owner/Executive Chef,
Eating Well with Chef Cordell

Don't ignore a gut feeling in an effort to make quick profit. All money is not good money. If your gut is telling you to walk away from an opportunity, you should. The same is true about negative people who do not support your vision. Avoid those types of people and situations like the plague.

LESSON #34

Don't Waste Time with Excuses

Matthew Lee, 'America's Homeownership and Wealth Expert'

Take personal responsibility for your mistakes, and don't concern yourself with what other people might say, thus, feel the necessity to come up with an excuse. If you make a mistake, own it and do not counter the experience by justifying the circumstances.

A business owner, who does not do that, will miss all of the lessons that can be learned from making a mistake, or failing. For example, so often people will make excuses, such as, 'the economy this, or the economy that.'

But what will you do the next time the economy slows down? If you continue do the same thing you were doing, before the economy slowed, instead of learning from the experience, you have to take personal responsibility for that. The experience from your initial failure serves as sign of things to come in your future.

In other words, if you choose to ignore the signs, take personal responsibility, and do not waste time blaming circumstances, the economy, or the people around you.

When you can have the humility to say, "I messed up," you'll be able to recognize and correct your shortcomings, learn from them, and move forward. When you decide to do this, you'll find that process is much faster than the time it takes to make excuses.

Sit down in a quiet space, and ask yourself, "Was I the root cause of this problem?" That exercise is the most powerful learning event any entrepreneur will ever experience.

I've never heard that there was a pre-requisite, to get approval from others, to move toward your dream.

~ Curtis Monday

LESSON #35

Avoid Dream Killers

Curtis Monday, Agent, State Farm Insurance

First, identify and then avoid the attackers who will come to destroy your entrepreneurial dream. Some individuals have goals or dreams, and they share them with others who cannot appreciate their vision. And the people they share with begin to discourage, because of their lack of appreciation.

Fortunately, I've never heard that there was a pre-requisite, to get approval from others, to move toward your dream. So it very important to avoid the tendency that some entrepreneurs have, which is an attempt to gain validation from others, to believe in their own dream.

I can remember when I shared with some family members that I was going to quit my corporate job, and start my own business. I had just finish graduate school, and many of my relatives said, "Why would you do that?" Now this was advice from my family, close relatives...people who had shaped and molded me. But it wasn't malicious, it was simply that I saw something they didn't see.

As an entrepreneur, it is important for you to realize you have rare gift to envision outcomes that others may not appreciate, or even comprehend at all.

LESSON #36

Don't be Afraid to Sing a Solo

Q. Scott Riley, CEO, New Guard Multimedia

What does Lionel Richie, Michael Jackson, and Beyonce' have in common? Well, in addition to a bunch of hit records, wealth, and fame. Each individual was not afraid to take center stage, and embrace the idea of a solo career. In other words, when the time arrived for them to leave the group, (for whatever reason) they made up their minds quickly, and did it.

Much like the three aforementioned musical superstars, so often, I've seen business owners start their entrepreneurial journey within a group or partnership. But as the business grows, they ignore the signs that indicate that the group effort will not be productive. Or simply, isn't in their best interest.

This reality is not always tied to a negative. But, be it positive, negative, or neutral. If there is a business problem that's bigger than the business plan, don't be afraid to leave.

I implore entrepreneurs to avoid the temptation of babysitting irrelevant troubles, or wasting time trying to resolve non-business related issues.

Being an entrepreneur means, that at any given time, you will be faced with multiple responsibilities that require your undivided attention.

Even after completing detailed research, raising adequate capital, and writing a strong business plan, owning a successful business can be an uphill battle.

Therefore, a serious entrepreneur has no time for indecisiveness, sloth, or drama on behalf of other individuals, within the business setting. There are times when entrepreneurs hesitate to leave a bad business partnership, often either because of the camaraderie that has developed, a prior friendship that existed, or family connections involved.

This dilemma will separate the boys from the men, and the girls from the women! Or, for that matter, the unsuccessful, from the successful. If you want to be a successful entrepreneur, you must subscribe to the theory, 'it's always business, never personal.'

If and when you are ever faced with this type of obstacle, continue to pursuit success as an entrepreneur, but reassess your plans, and commitments.

And if necessary, muster the courage to sing a solo.

LESSON #37

Don't Automatically Discount Your Market Value

**Chef Cordell McGary, II Owner/Executive Chef,
Eating Well with Chef Cordell**

Many entrepreneurs, particularly those that are new to business ownership, have the tendency to automatically discount the value of their place in the market. However, before automatically doing this, take some time and determine what your services or products are really worth to the market?

Do not be timid. Ask yourself, 'how much does the competition charge for a similar product?' And just maybe, as a newcomer, you won't ask for the same price as your more established competition, initially. But be careful not discount your market value by a large percentage, such as 50%. Your prices should reflect the quality you offer, and should not be substantially lower than what market rate will bare, simply because you're new. I would suggest a 5-10% discount, just long enough for your brand to become established.

LESSON #38

Avoid Working in a Bubble

Richard White II, CEO, Black Eagle Marketing, Inc.

Do not isolate yourself. As soon as you can, attempt to get others involved in what you are doing. Take time to find out who your market competitors are, and if possible, learn from them. Study how they are making a living and mimic, yet enhance or restructure their efforts as you create a sustainable business.

LESSON #39

Take Off the Blinders

Curtis Monday, Agent, State Farm Insurance

A tactical mistake that entrepreneurs should avoid is working in a silo. This particularly happens during the early years of business ownership. Too often, during this stage, we tend to work full-speed-ahead, with blinders on.

We don't leverage relationships, and sometimes we just move forward, without ever looking at other successful business models. Furthermore, we are too often not open and receptive to information from others, which can cause us to miss the advantage of possible mentorship.

LESSON #40

Never Jeopardize Your Reputation

DeAnna McLeary, Founder/Executive Director, True Star Foundation

As entrepreneurs we are natural salespersons. We know how to do the dog and pony show, and we know how to put the glitter on the dirt. But be very careful not to make promises that you cannot deliver to investors, customers, landlords, employees, etc. Your name will proceed in you in business. So never do anything to jeopardize your reputation.

People trust you when others say that you are a person who can deliver. So, always go above and beyond for your clients, and other people who believe and trust in you.

But, nevertheless, I so often see entrepreneurs pouting and throwing tantrums with their clients. I look at that and ask them, "How does that help your brand?"

Therefore, keep in mind; never take anything personal in business. As an entrepreneur, I understand your business, might be your baby. But don't take things personal. And if you can't resist the temptation of taking a situation personal, find a trustworthy friend, and vent to that person until you get over it.

You don't want to burn your bridges, because the person that pissed you off today may be in charge of your biggest account tomorrow. So don't do anything that can compromise your integrity, and be sure to protect your relationships.

LESSON #41

Don't Borrow for the Sake of Borrowing

Warren Dobson, Dobson Products

If you are going to borrow money, make sure you have a clear plan how the money will be used. Never borrow money, for the sake of borrowing. Because you have to keep in mind, the day will soon come upon you, when you will have to repay the loan.

In addition, make sure you know whether it's best to borrow a loan, secure a line of credit, or raise capital by offering equity to investors.

LESSON #42

Do Not Invest in Property over People

DeAnna McLeary, Founder/Executive Director, True Star Foundation

I know an agency that gained one really big client, and immediately moved from a small office that was meeting the needs of the business, into a much larger office nearly three sizes bigger. And within a matter of months, they were laying off over half of their staff.

I knew exactly what was happening. They were struggling to pay the increased rent for that new and bigger office space. After seeing that, I vowed not make that mistake.

Never make big moves until you know you'll have the cash flow. Do not believe the hype that you always have to look the part, before you make it. For example, people will suggest, "you need to have a fancy office in the business district of your city, for the purpose of your company's image." Hell, no! That is not true for most businesses.

I've seen a lot of entrepreneurs invest too much capital in property over people. You don't need the bells and whistles, unless you need the bells and whistles.

Networking is never optional.

~ Monika Simmons

Lesson #43

Networking is Not Optional

Arika and Monika Simmons, Double Stitch

(Monika Simmons) Networking should not be taking lightly. In fact, networking is never optional. There are many entrepreneurs who feel they don't need to network. However, in order to succeed and grow your business, you will need others. The good thing about that is, people want to know you. So start networking, immediately...real live networking.

And always think about what your business can do for others: customers, other business owners, etc. If you have the attitude, 'what can I do to help others?' You will always find that your business needs will be met.

Genuine relationships are very important for your brand. It doesn't matter what you're selling, customers can likely buy that product from another business.

However, the thing that will make the big difference is when people know about you. When they know who you are, and know your story.

LESSON #44

Don't Shoot From the Hip

Ms. Dana, Owner, The Loctician and Barber Studio

You have to see it, before you can believe it! For that reason, I think the vision board, is the simplest most magnificent concept ever. You have to write down your vision and make it plain. It is important to gather words, pictures, lists, and spreadsheets, and keep it out in front of you.

Even if all you want is a lemonade stand, you have to put it on paper. 'How much is it going cost you to build the stand? Where will we buy lemons? How much is the sugar? How much are the tops for cups, so people don't spill their drink? What will be our selling price for lemonade? Is there a profit margin?' You have to put all of those things in front of you.

A lot of people who are not business owners, and who never have been, will encourage you not to do that.

But, as an entrepreneur, you can't take advice from employee-minded people, regarding business ownership matters. You simply cannot do it.

You have to get advice from someone who is already doing it, and preferably, someone who is willing to be transparent and speak on their failures, too. Because we will all fail. It's almost required.

However, there are some things we fail at as entrepreneurs that are due to just shooting from the hip. When you shoot from the hip, you will fail far more often than you have to, and when you're down, you will most likely stay there.

LESSON #45

Avoid Assumptions...Take Classes

Arika and Monika Simmons, Double Stitch

(Arika Simmons) Do not assume in certain areas of your business, i.e., tax laws, finance, and administration. We could have done better, in terms of doing research on hiring professional service providers, such as accountants, attorneys, etc.

If you are an artist, as I am, it will only help to come out of your comfort zone and learn as much as you can about all aspects of the business.

I suggest entrepreneurs take classes in the areas where they are weak. And don't assume that all hired professionals know everything they should know for the best interest of your business.

For example, request that your accountant explain all of your company's tax matters to you, on terms that you understand. As opposed to someone just telling you to do this, or to do that.

Although you want qualified professionals, you want to understand as much as you can personally. You don't want to get lost focusing only on the part of the business that comes naturally to you.

LESSON #46

Avoid Inadequate Finances

Jason Caston, CEO, Caston Digital LLC

I would always suggest that entrepreneurs should avoid launching a venture, without having any sort of financial backing. It is a mistake I have witness many entrepreneurs make.

When a business does not have adequate finances, the company may not have money when the time arrives to hire service professionals, to get your name out in the marketplace with websites, advertising, etc.

This problem can cause the business to look and perform, less than professional. And can be the determining factor behind whether or not a customer chooses to patronize your business.

LESSON #47

Avoid the Free-Work Trap

Tiffany Jasper, CEO, Tiff's Editing Cafe

There are so many times as entrepreneurs, we want to help customers who are having financial issues. Fortunately, we have every right to pick and choose who we bless with our charitable services.

However, it is so easy to get stuck in that frame of mind to "help." Before you know it, you are providing nothing but free services, losing a lot of time, and making no financial gain.

So, I choose twice a month, how I will bless a client with a free service. Other than that, I will have to charge, even if it is a payment arrangement.

LESSON #48

Do not Let Success Take You by Surprise

Jason Caston, CEO, Caston Digital LLC

Many of us think we are prepared for success. But what if someone approached you today and said, "I want to buy your product or service. And I'm going to give you a million dollar contract." Could you meet that demand? So often, the problem is, many business owners could not.

Almost all entrepreneurs think they want to make a lot of money, but what they don't think about is, 'How will the profits be used?' 'What is our accounting process?' 'What is the distribution processes?' 'What will be the manpower required to meet a multimillion dollar contract?'

Do not find yourself unprepared for what success really looks like when it shows up. Therefore, be prepared, have systems in place, and don't let success take you by surprise.

Lesson #49

Avoid Unrelated Product Extensions

Warren Dobson, Dobson Products

The one thing that I hear a lot of entrepreneurs say is that they want 'multiple streams of income.' I can agree with that if they are in related businesses.

I have multiple streams of income, but I only go after business that is within the various niches of my industry.

For instance, early in my business career, I was heavily into selling my products as a wholesaler. And then eventually, I began to focus more on selling products as a retailer. But it was all related to the same business, and even the same brand.

In addition, even if I had expanded into custom designs, it would have still been inter-related to the clothing design business that I own.

However, on the other hand, let's say I'm an insurance agent, and in addition, I sell real estate, and also own a fried chicken restaurant on the side. The insurance and real estate can work together, but the chicken restaurant doesn't fit well into the model.

I have seen many entrepreneurs dabble into various unrelated streams of income, and don't do well. Sadly, most that choose this approach only do so, because they've been sold on the concept, and not because it is a proven method.

LESSON #50

Learn to Delegate

Jason Caston, CEO, Caston Digital LLC

Too many business owners try to do everything themselves. They start off right, doing what they are good at doing. For example, let's say you are one of the best widget makers, ever. That's Great! But do not try to do all of the other aspects of the business that you are not qualified to do.

This will mean your business will have great widgets, but nobody will get to use the product, because the marketing of the business is so bad that the customers will not even consider making a purchase.

Focus on what you're good at doing. Don't try to be the website master, the accountant, and every other aspect of your business, because you may not be good at that. Instead, delegate those things. That will keep the business running smoothly, and professionally.

Lesson #51

Avoid Immeasurable Marketing

Warren Dobson, Dobson Products

Marshall Fields once said, "I know that half of my marketing efforts are working, I just don't know which half."

Make sure all of your marketing efforts are measurable. For example, if you're distributing flyers, or brochures, make sure that each piece in traceable, and incentivizes the prospective customer with a reason to contact the business. At the point of contact, you can measure your efforts.

LESSON #52

Avoid Being Uninformed and Misinformed

Sherman Wright, Co-Founder/Managing Partner, Common Ground

The one mistake I would advise business owners to avoid is being uninformed or misinformed. As smart as you think you are, after you launch your business, and you're out there all alone, you may realize that your plan was not as well thought out as you initially figured.

You don't want to discover that you are under-resourced in the area of business-intelligence, and that you're operating in a mode of 'learn as you go.' Successful business ownership goes far beyond when you open your doors for operation. It's really much more about doing your homework before you launch.

PART III

RECOVERY

"Don't just think outside the box... remove the box!"

~ Shaniqua Jones

RECOVERY

Former Heavyweight Boxing Champ, Mike Tyson once said, "Every fighter has a plan...until they get punched in the nose." Fortunately, in the sport of boxing, the greatness of a fighter is not measured by the number of times he is knocked down. But by the number of times he gets back up.

Moreover, the response a fighter exhibits after getting back to his feet offers an even more believable forecast.

The same principle applies for entrepreneurship. As an entrepreneur, we all have a plan, until we get hit in the face with unexpected challenges.

This book would be benefit no one if I chose to sugar-coat, and diminish the potential challenge and complexities that are associated with owning and operating a business. Many times as business owners we get knocked down so fast, and so hard, we find ourselves figuratively lying on our backs, gasping for our next breath. And some of our biggest defeats are, though unintended, often self-induced.

'If I only knew then, what I know now' has become a battle cry for thousands of business owners. Whether they are seasoned, or novice; successful, or unsuccessful. Their choices, plans, and decisions, will make or break their operation. In the famous words of the character, *Hyman Roth*, from *The Godfather II,* "This is the business we've chosen."

In Lesson #69 of this book, Attorney and entrepreneur, Shara Kamal, admonishes the reader to "Get Comfortable with the Roller Coaster Ride." But what if the ride is too fast for us to stop, think, and re-trace out steps. Never giving us a chance to say to ourselves, "Why did I do that?" "And if I had the chance, what would I change?"

The grim reality of this scenario is, neither life, nor business ever seems to slow down enough for us to assess past choices. We are constantly looking for the next sale, or pursuing new clients, or managing personnel, all the while hoping we can make payroll on Friday.

And as we navigate through this labor of love, called entrepreneurship. We continuously hear a voice in our head saying, "If I could only go back in time and apply all of the things I learned over the years, to this business, when it was launched. Just how successful could I be today?"

But we ignore that voice. Because time travel doesn't exist in our world. So why bother.

Here is more good news. No, I did not create a method of time-travel.

Yet, I did give individuals a platform to reflect on their business ownership careers, and enter a world (if only make-believe and temporary) where they were able to reflect on their past, and pick which business decisions they would eliminate, keep, and adjust.
Or, in the words of entrepreneur, Jason Caston, "I wouldn't change a thing!"

Part III of this book, *Recovery*, offers the reader a rare look at hindsight business hints from individuals who have experienced both success and failure as entrepreneurs.

These candid testimonies illustrate how successful business owners were able to continue operations despite the climate of their conditions. Each experienced failure, discovered success, and managed to recover, again, and again...

Twenty-four successful urban entrepreneurs were interviewed and asked, 'In hindsight, if given the opportunity, are there any business-ownership choices or decisions that you would do differently?'

In hindsight, if given the opportunity, are there any business-ownership choices or decisions that you would do differently?

LESSON #53

Prioritize Paperwork, Processes, and Partnerships

DeAnna McLeary, Founder/Executive Director, True Star Foundation

If I was to offer a hindsight hint to business owners, from the technical perspective of an entrepreneur. I would say to be diligent about paperwork, processes, partnerships, and legalities. Those things come with price tags, and mistakes in business can cost the business owner lots of money.

Entrepreneurs should do as much research as possible, within their professional network to establish if there is someone in your circles, who can offer legal expertise. And if possible, find anyone who is aware of pro bono legal services.

I would also advise anyone who is planning to work with a business partner, to make sure their partner will compliment their skill set.

Business partnerships are very much like marriages. Therefore, you need to know if that person can stand the test of time with you. 'Will they stand with you, when you can't make payroll?' 'Do they mirror your work ethic?' 'Do they match your passion?'

Furthermore, all entrepreneurs are to be very mindful that there is a big difference between being self employed, and being a business owner.

For example, if the CEO of large corporation decided to leave the company, the business operations continue, because there are systems, policies, and procedures in place to maintain production.

Therefore, it is very important to create solid business processes within the venture, as early as possible.

So often within entrepreneurship, we hear so much about the importance of a business plan. But as a business owner, I submit that the stronger your processes are, and the sooner they are implemented, the less you will have to worry when change within the business happens.

I have had many employees come and go. But as a business environment changes, as well as personnel, you will need to have reliable company processes in place to handle operations such as revenue, personnel, and growth.

When you create a strong process, you won't be moved or rattled by change. Because you've created a machine that works.

LESSON #54

Learn How to Properly Assess Your Company's Revenue

Joshua Mercer, Owner, Allstate Insurance Agency

I have one hint to offer in hindsight, that I would share with any entrepreneur. 'Definitely know how your business makes money.' Strive to achieve beyond the little milestone profits. Never settle—the idea is to grow, sell, or pass the business on in some type of legacy.

If I could do it over again, I would take business leadership classes that instruct on making solid business decisions that are not based on emotions. It is also good to have benchmarks in place to measure your definition of success and profitability.

And, I would also take a finance course, to better understand earnings, monthly income statements, and balance sheets. Those classes will help an entrepreneur clearly see and understand where the company's money is being spent.

Many times, business owners close lots of transactions, but they may not profit as much as they think. For instance, let's say you're planning to hire a public relations professional to create a new promotion campaign for your company.

It is a good idea to sit with an accountant first, review the books, and determine the financial priorities of the business. So that you're not putting the company at risk to experience negative cash flow at a later time.

LESSON #55

Nurture Your Brand

Julie Holloway, President, JMH Art & Design

My helpful hint is to break your brand into parts, and learn how to market each part. Then never stop marketing your brand. Morning, noon, and night.

I have a quote that I came up with somewhere along the journey, "If you stop marketing, then they stop watching." I say that from experience, because I love what I do: graphic design.

I go through periods, sometimes weeks, where I'm just very busy and bogged down with all of the projects that I have taken on, and I forget to market. But if you forget to market, the market will forget you.

There is no sales activity when you forget to market, other than customers who know you personally. What I noticed, after I did this the first time, is when I came up for air, and got back in the swing of marketing, the leads started coming in.

I begin hearing from old clients again, and even receiving new proposals. In other words, when I started marketing again, after a break in activity, that's when I saw the activity in revenue.

So, I truly feel if you stop marketing, people will stop buying. Because they are missing your brand presence.

Lesson #56

Make Good Use of Technology: Early and Often

Warren Dobson, Dobson Products

When I started my business, I refused to use a computer to manage certain operations, such as maintaining records, creating invoices, handling accounting transactions, etc.

Many entrepreneurs, particularly in the early stages of business ownership, make that same mistake. So, my helpful hint in hindsight is, 'step out of the dark ages' and don't be stubborn.

Use the tools that are available in the market. They will enable you to brand yourself better. And, will make life easier, and give any small business a more professional look.

LESSON #57

Work in the Business, as Well as on the Business

Curtis Monday, Agent, State Farm Insurance

I've been a business owner for 13 years. And my experience has been excellent. But, there are some things I would name as a do-over. First, when I started my agency, I spent too much time just doing. Often times as entrepreneurs, we possess certain skills that we do well.

But translating those skills into business can be tough. There is more to owning a business than what you do. For example, the core of my business is insurance and financial services. So in the beginning, I spent most of my time hustling, and selling policies.

But I spent very little, to no time at all; developing the model I wanted my business look like in the future. Nor did I spend anytime reviewing business financials, such as cash flow projections, ROI, profit/loss statements, or growth strategies.

Consequently, I earned a lot of business. But I ran into many growing pains that I could have avoided, if I had spent more time, working in the business, as well as, on the business.

If I could do it all over again, I would spend more time on developing strategy to grow the business, and utilizing technology and resources that are available to help operate the business.

LESSON #58

Maintain a Business Coach During Growth Seasons

Tiffany Jasper, CEO, Tiff's Editing Cafe

If I could do it all over again, I would have maintained the services of my business coach, even after I saw initial results. After my business secured its first clients and profits, I had no direction. I was just doing whatever was requested of me, which didn't work most times.

I've learned that it is important to continue to work with a business coach or mentor, through the first growth season. Not only will you receive ideas about how to manage the growth of the new business. You will also gain the benefit of support, as you implement new ideas at the next level.

Lesson #59

Plan, Save, and Prepare Early

Sherman Wright, Co-Founder/Managing Partner, Common Ground

If I could go back, and start my business over again. I would start by saving, planning, and preparing a lot earlier in the process than I did.

Prior to starting my business, I worked hard to put away as much money as I could, in an effort to have a great foundation when I started. And we still found that we were under-capitalized at times.

It's important to think a lot about what it's going to take to start your business, specifically from a capitalization standpoint. I think the most important thing, for any business that you start, is capitalization and finding out what that means for you.

LESSON #60

Embrace the Process

Jason Caston, CEO, Caston Digital, LLC

Honestly, if I could it all over again, I wouldn't change anything. The reason I say that is because there are too many young, new entrepreneurs who don't want to embrace the process.

Many of us want success, but we don't want to put in the long hours to get there. If it takes 10,000 hours of dedicated learning, experience, and education to become an expert in your field, then you want the process to be at least 10,000 hours. If not more. That is the type of expertise as an entrepreneur, you want to have.

My journey has been quite adventurous. I have learned to live in the moment, and work through the pitfalls and short comings. But each one of those events has molded me into the person I am today. If I could go back and change things, then my outcome would be different, and I wouldn't want that. Nope, I wouldn't change a thing.

LESSON #61

Let Experience Be Your Trophy

Adam Jackson, 'America's Implementation Expert'

I don't believe I would be who I am today, if I had not made the mistakes I made yesterday. As entrepreneurs, our experiences, good or bad, have brought us to where we are. I embrace the missed opportunities, and failures that I have experienced. For example, I recall one day driving down the street, and I passed by a bus stop where a beautiful young lady was standing. We made eye-contact, and there was an undeniable energy. And then, the light changed.

The cars behind me began to blow their horns, and I had to drive away. I made three immediate right turns, in effort to return to that stop. However, when I reached the spot, the bus had arrived, and was pulling away with the pretty lady. I followed that bus for nearly two miles, only to discover the lady was not on the bus. 'Where did she go,' I thought. At that moment, I felt that was such a missed opportunity. Wow! Just the vibe we shared from our first look generated such favorable potential.

But, if I had met that lady, and if I had not experienced missed opportunity and disappointment, I would not have the thing that presently inspires me more than anything in the world: My family and kids.

The same principle is true in business for entrepreneurs. I've learned to embrace all situations we encounter in business, as we must in life. The fact is, the young lady was actually a missed opportunity. But your actuality does not have to become your reality.
The bad things that you go through is not who you are. The important thing is that we gain answers, as we reach the other side of the experience. My trophy is experience. What I cherish the most about entrepreneurship is the anticipation of the things that haven't even happen yet. That makes me excited more than anything.

LESSON #62

Take Yourself Seriously from the Start

Monique Caradine, President, Momentum Media

I have been in business for 10 years, and entrepreneurship has been an incredible journey. But if I could talk to my 33-year-old self, which is when I decided to go into business, there are a couple of things I would do differently.

First, I would take myself more seriously from the start. I went into business because I was mad that I couldn't get a raise at work. I was working at a radio station at the time. So I really started my company out of spite, and did not know if this thing was going to work or not. I just said, "Forget them."

In hindsight, I should have done a lot more research. Then I could have been far more strategic about getting into the marketplace. Thus, I could have charged higher rates.

Secondly, I would sit down to create a plan, a strategy, a forecast, and a vision for the business. I would take the time to determine how my unique brilliance, could offer value to the market.

If I had done those couple of things, I would have avoided a lot of mistakes.

LESSON #63

Identify Your Strengths

Julie Holloway, President, JMH Art & Design

As a thought in hindsight, I would tell an entrepreneur to identify the passion and purpose that drives you to own and operate a business. And from that effort, start to identify your strengths. Make sure you don't try to do everything yourself, because you will only dig yourself into a deep hole.

I've learned to stay in my lane. I am a graphic artist, so I do graphic design. I know that my strong suit is not finance and bookkeeping. Trying to wear too many hats at one time is a recipe for disaster.

Next, immediately begin to develop professional relationships with appropriate experts, and begin outsourcing to service providers, the work you can't personally handle, and don't wish to manage. Identify, and remove those things off your plate from the start.

LESSON #64

Know Your Weaknesses

Joshua Mercer, Owner, Allstate Insurance Agency

Define your weaknesses! As an entrepreneur, you cannot identify your business needs, until you first define your personal weaknesses.

At that point, you can determine if the business needs support in the areas of capital, human resource, or elsewhere.

LESSON #65

Seek Investments of Capital and Expertise

Chef Cordell McGary II, Owner/Executive Chef, Eating Well with Chef Cordell

Though I regret nothing, if I could do anything over again, I would seek outside investors. Using OPM (other people's money), is a safe method of capital development that will not deplete your personal finances.

I would seek a pool of qualified investors, and assure each investor has expertise in areas of business where I lack knowledge.

Having a passion and a dream is good. However, using OPM in an effort to bring a dream to fruition, is great.

LESSON #66

Learn the Business of the Business

Richard White II, CEO, Black Eagle Marketing, Inc.

I evolved into an entrepreneur without even knowing exactly what it meant. Honestly, owning and running a business wasn't my vision. And it probably isn't for many people. So, if I could do it all over again, I would take business management courses.

As a student, I was taught the fundamentals of my craft. But I did not learn how to manage clients, conduct market research, or how to determine the growth of a business.

In other words, learn the business of the business. Aside from that suggestion, the only other way to learn how to properly operate your business is by trial and error.

LESSON #67

Hire Slowly and Fire Quickly

**DeAnna McLeary, Founder/Executive Director,
True Star Foundation**

In business ownership, human resources are very critical. So, when employees show you who they are, believe them. If people are not performing, you cannot afford to keep them as a part of your team.

Do not adopt the frame of mind, that you won't be able to replace a person. All employees are replaceable. However, often times in small business environments, the staff becomes very 'family-like.' And what happens as a result is the family becomes hard to fire.

But, in hindsight, I have been burned so many times giving people second and third opportunities, after telling myself the first time, 'I need to terminate that person.' Every person I tried to hang on to as an employee after I initially said I should let them go; I was burned later when I didn't.

Hiring and firing is the hardest thing that you'll ever do in business, but, it is the nature of entrepreneurship. But if you do both well, you'll be better off.

LESSON #68

Focus on Staff Development

L. Brian Jenkins, Founder and President, Starting Up Now Business Solutions, Inc.

In hindsight, one of the things I would do different as an entrepreneur is focus more time on building the proper team. I've learned that the key thing in terms of building the right business team is to make sure everyone knows the corporate direction of the company.

With that being said, be very careful who you invite to serve on your team, at every level, from the board, to the staff.

Also, make sure that everyone can negate their own personal egos in an effort to accomplish the corporate goal. Be sure that everyone has similar values, and based on those values; develop a shared-value system. If these things are firmly in place, your team will support you as the team leader, in relation to revenue, effort, and time. However, you have to be cautious who is on your team. You don't want someone adding too many personal ideas to your vision. As an entrepreneur, you want people on your team, who will add value, without getting in your way.

LESSON #69

Create a Standard Operating Procedure

Q. Scott Riley, CEO, New Guard Multimedia

When I think about business hints in hindsight, I'm reminded of the character from the movie *Coming to America, Cleo McDowell*. This man is the owner of a fast-food, burger operation that eerily looks and operates like McDonald's. Throughout the movie, he is caught several times studying a McDonald's franchise manual in his effort to replicate the success of his more established, industry competitor.

Although the story is fiction, and in real life, this would be a major infraction on the rights of a Fortune 500 corporation, and grounds for a law suit. However, if I could do it all over again the theory is a practice I would use myself.

I've often taught my business students and clients, to McDonald-ize their business. In other words, create a SOP (standard operating procedure). A SOP is basically a manual of written processes that employees, managers, and owners use as a standard for every area of the business.

This is particularly critical for entrepreneurs in the area of customer service and receipt of payment. Think about the smooth and simple process a customer experiences when ordering service at McDonald's. 1) The menu clearly presents products the company offers. 2) The customer selects their order. 3) The customer pays, the full amount, for the purchase. 4) The customer receives their selection upon payment...simple! That is a SOP.

As a business owner, many times in the past, I experienced being haggled, missing a sale, very late payments, or even no payment for services rendered, due to the fact that my business did have an established SOP.

LESSON #70

Find Secure Mentors

Carl Ankrum, The Media MD.com

If I could do it all over again, I would seek out some existing small business owners and get some solid advice. You can never discount learning from the growing pains of a more experienced entrepreneur. And they do not have to own a company in your same industry. There are so many aspects of all small businesses that are the same.

For example, the process of creating a proper pricing structure, or developing compensation package for you, as a business owner.

Many entrepreneurs start a business with out having a clue how to do either. I know now, that I should have picked a particular company that is similar to my business, and studied their model.

I encourage any entrepreneur to focus on what they really want to do, and find someone who has already accomplished it. And talk to that person about what they do, and how they do it.

But, you need to find the right person. If you're not careful, you may find someone who is insecure, and who feels you're going to compete with them. They are not going to help you, and may even try to harm your efforts in some sort of way.

So often, insecure people will tell you that the market is saturated. "We don't need anyone else in the market: We don't need anymore lawyers...We don't need anymore graphic designers, or writers, or accountants, etc."

But, I can't recall how many times I've seen a CVS Pharmacy across the street from a Walgreens; or a KFC across the street from a Popeye's Chicken. So don't be discouraged by insecure people.

The key is, to find secure mentors, who are not threaten by your potential. Afterwards, find your niche in the market, and figure out how to do it differently, and hopefully better than the competition.

I say to my business, "If in the past, I had given you the attention you deserved, where might we be right now?"

~ Sean Hicks

LESSON #71

Give Your Business the Attention it Deserves

**Sean Hicks, Principal/Chief Creative Officer,
Gargoyle Creative Designs**

Like many entrepreneurs, I didn't have a plan. I actually fell into my business. My mentor offered me an opportunity to do some work on the side, in addition to the full-time job I had, and it worked out well. Eventually, word of mouth kicked in, and one day I looked up and realized I had this asset that was generating a steady stream of income.

But even then, I didn't give it the respect I should have. Therefore, my biggest entrepreneurial do-over, is that I would actually put the horse before the cart, and pay more attention to the business. I would also develop a business plan around my initial opportunity. My first 10-12 years as an entrepreneur, I treated my business like a side-mistress. I only paid attention to her when she was acting right, and I didn't pay any attention to her when it wasn't fun.

At that time, my plan was to reach all of my goals as an employee...and then life changed: marriage, a home, kids, and then my perspective changed, too.

I thought, "Hey, I have something that has actually helped me to sustain for years. What would happen, if I gave this thing some serious attention?" So I decided to pay more attention to the thing I was considering to be just a side show, or hobby. I've learn to make her my number #1 priority; my main interest!

I realized that when I gave my business the attention it deserved, it began to really grow. And at this point, I say to my business, "If in the past, I had given you the attention you deserved, where might we be right now?"

LESSON #72

Get Comfortable with the Roller Coaster Ride

Attorney Shara Kamal, Founder/Managing Attorney, When Fashion Meets Law, PC

I've been practicing law for 12 years, and early in my practice, I put all of my eggs in one business basket--real estate law. And when the market was booming in that sector of the economy, I had upwards of 200-300 real estate closings per year. It was great! I upgraded all of my systems, hired a full-time assistant, and secured a larger office.

But in hindsight, I probably spent more business revenue than I should have. I had not factored in what would happen if the market slowed down. So, when the real estate sector took a downward turn, I had to quickly diversify the legal services that my firm offered. But in the midst of switching my company's focus, I still had the higher rent for the bigger office. And I still had to pay the salaries for the increased staff. I now know that I should have saved more of the company's revenue, for a rainy day. Because the rainy days will come.

Therefore, I would say if could do it all over again, I would save as much of the company's profits as possible, and I would encourage any entrepreneur to do the same.

As an entrepreneur, you will experience ups and downs in any business; it is a roller coaster ride. The important thing is to save company revenue, and prepare yourself to get comfortable with the ride.

LESSON #73

Understand the Trinity of Taxation

Greg Pipkin, Owner, Suburban Tees and Sports

My hint to business owners is to have a good understanding of taxes when they start. When you are a hobbyist, and the business is not your main source of income, taxes are the furthest thing from your mind.

But after the business grows and you incorporate the operation, taxes will rank up there as one of your top business priorities. At the start of a business, you may not worry about collecting a sales tax with every purchase. When an entrepreneur starts small, tax is a responsibility...as the business grows, it becomes a liability!!

Thus, there are three phases of taxes to which a business owner should pay close attention. 1) Is charging taxes at the appropriate rate. 2) Setting up a process to charge and collect taxes for every transaction. 3) As a retailer, the monthly, quarterly, and annual federal sales tax report.

Many entrepreneurs manage their own taxes and books early on. But as soon as possible, hire a good accountant and record keeper, and that can take you a long way.

LESSON #74

Surround Yourself with People who Have What You Want

Ms. Dana, Owner, The Loctician and Barber Studio

I actually started my entrepreneurial journey in my 20's. But I procrastinated and I was working afraid. I researched things to death, but I never moved on it. I just continued to operate out of fear.

So, if I could do it over again, I would find a successful business owner who would be willing to give me a conversation over breakfast once a month. I would be prepared to use that time wisely, and have three solid questions ready that I need answered.

I would also change the people I hang with. Not just in terms of mentors, but the people I socialize with, as well. There is nothing wrong with having life-long friends, but you have to add those people who already have what you want, to your social calendar.

Initiate times to socially interact with a group of business owners. A weekend breakfast, a shopping outing, or a night out with three or four entrepreneurs. You may be surprised to find out how much you'll share with each other about business within those social gatherings.

Surround yourself with the people who are doing what you want to do, and that have what you want, and who are going where you want to go!

I believe the universe places stumbling blocks in your path, with the intent for them to later become stepping stones.

~ DeAnna McLeary

LESSON #75

Turn Your Stumbling Blocks, into Stepping Stones

DeAnna McLeary, Founder/Executive Director, True Star Foundation

I typically don't think about things in reference to doing them differently. Because I come from the school of thought that says, 'every mistake happens for a reason.' I believe the universe places stumbling blocks in your path, with the intent for them to later become stepping stones. So from the visionary perspective of a business owner, I wouldn't change anything.

I believe every failure, and every mistake helped me reach the next level. I would not be the person I am, or where I am, without those experiences.

Connect with us
online at
www.UrbanBizVideo.com

www.ingramcontent.com/pod-product-compliance
Lightning Source LLC
Chambersburg PA
CBHW060559200326
41521CB00007B/617